Medications and Surgeries for Weight Loss:
When Dieting Isn't Enough

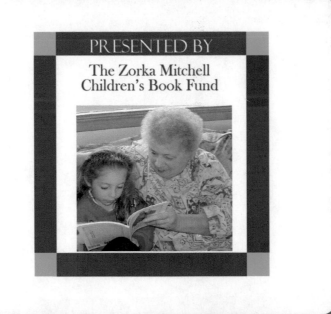

Obesity: Modern-Day Epidemic

Medications and Surgeries for Weight Loss:
When Dieting Isn't Enough

by
William Hunter

Mason Crest Publishers
Philadelphia

First printing
1 2 3 4 5 6 7 8 9 10
          Library of Congress Cataloging-in-Publication Data

Hunter, William, 1971–
  Medications and surgeries for weight loss : when dieting isn't enough / by
William Hunter.
      p. cm. — (Obesity : modern day epidemic)
  Includes index.
  ISBN 1-59084-947-7— ISBN 1-59084-941-8 (series)
  1. Weight loss. 2. Obesity. I. Title. II. Obesity (Philadelphia, Pa.)
  RM222.2.H864 2005
  616.3'980654—dc22
                              2004022956

Produced by Harding House Publishing Service, Inc., Vestal, New York.
Cover design by Michelle Bouch.
Interior design by Michelle Bouch and MK Bassett-Harvey
Printed in the Hashemite Kingdom of Jordan.

Contents

Introduction

We as a society often reserve our harshest criticism for those conditions we understand the least. Such is the case with obesity. Obesity is a chronic and often-fatal disease that accounts for 400,000 deaths each year. It is second only to smoking as a cause of premature death in the United States. People suffering from obesity need understanding, support, and medical assistance. Yet what they often receive is scorn.

Today, children are the fastest growing segment of the obese population in the United States. This constitutes a public health crisis of enormous proportions. Living with childhood obesity affects self-esteem, employment, and attainment of higher education. But childhood obesity is much more than a social stigma. It has serious health consequences.

Childhood obesity increases the risk for poor health in adulthood and premature death. Depression, diabetes, asthma, gallstones, orthopedic diseases, and other obesity-related conditions are all on the rise in children. Recent estimates suggest that 30 to 50 percent of children born in 2000 will develop type 2 diabetes mellitus—a leading cause of preventable blindness, kidney failure, heart disease, stroke, and amputations. Obesity is undoubtedly the most pressing nutritional disorder among young people today.

This series is an excellent first step toward understanding the obesity crisis and profiling approaches for remedying it. If we are to reverse obesity's current trend, there must be family, community, and national objectives promoting healthy eating and exercise. As a nation, we must demand broad-based public-health initiatives to limit TV watching, curtail junk food advertising toward children, and promote physical activity. More than rhetoric, these need to be our rallying cry. Anything short of this will eventually fail, and within our lifetime obesity will become the leading cause of death in the United States if not in the world.

Victor F. Garcia, M.D.
Founder, Bariatric Surgery Center
Cincinnati Children's Hospital Medical Center
Professor of Pediatrics and Surgery
School of Medicine
University of Cincinnati

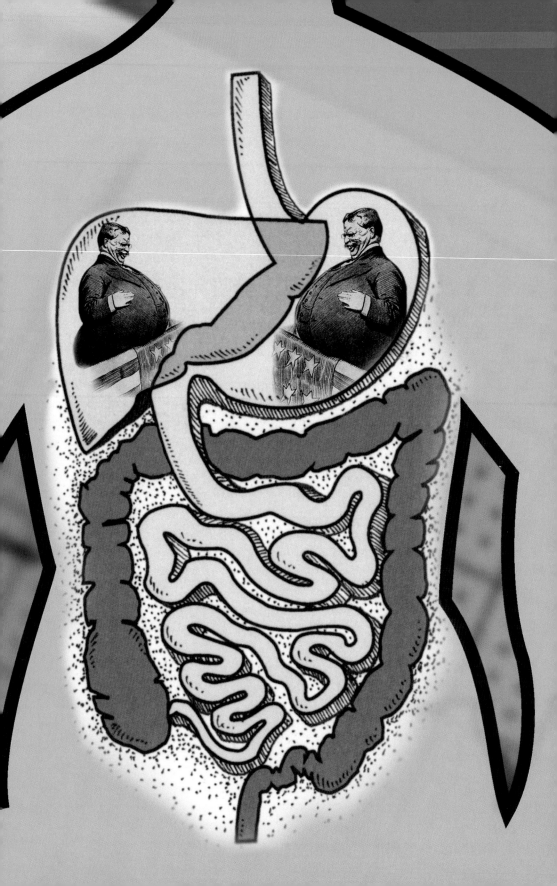

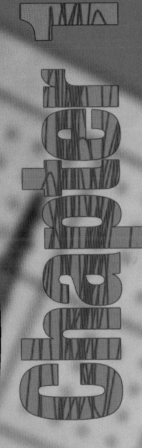

Chapter 1

What's Obesity All About? An Overview

Obesity is a hot topic. Over the past two decades, the numbers of obese and overweight individuals have climbed higher and higher. The medical costs of these skyrocketing numbers cause great concern. Obesity has become an *epidemic*.

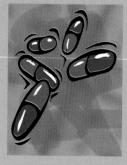

The History of Obesity

The 1990s were a decade of mixed messages: on the one hand, the cultural pressure to achieve the "perfect body" led to a surge in eating disorders such as *anorexia nervosa* and *bulimia*; on the other hand, ironically, food portion sizes grew rapidly, while at the same time, manufacturers produced more and more foods with large amounts of corn syrup and processed flour—foods that were high in calories but low in nutrition. Whether dieting or overeating, people had become fixated on food.

According to a report issued by the United States Centers for Disease Control and Prevention, in the last thirty years, the average caloric intake of an adult woman has grown by 335 calories per day; men take in about 168

Obesity is an international problem. Worldwide, more than one billion people are considered overweight, and at least three hundred million of these are obese.

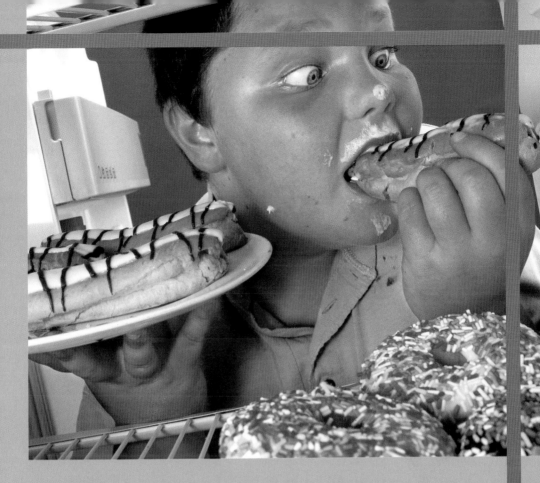

If the current trends continue, 100 percent of the U.S. population will be obese by the year 2230.

In the United States, the incidence of obesity among teenagers has nearly tripled since 1970.

more calories each day. On average, people eat about 1,775 pounds of food per year, up from 1,497 pounds in 1970. An increase in physical activity over the same time span would have greatly lessened the effect of the increase in food intake, but the last few decades have seen a decrease in physical activity as the age of computers and office jobs has changed the way people work and play across the country. For example, the problem is so severe that between 1971 and 2000 the percentage of Americans considered obese increased from 14.5 percent to almost 31 percent.

In response to this increase in obesity, the number of companies dealing with weight reduction has grown across the world. Among the most popular are programs such as Weight Watchers, Nutri-Systems, and Atkins. Programs like these have been very successful at selling their products to consumers. Dieting is big business.

Did you know that your concept of "fat" has a lot to do with your culture? In some countries, great value is placed on large body size. In others, small bodies are regarded with high esteem. Society has a great deal to do with the body type preferred among the population. Poor countries tend to see greater amounts of body fat as a sign of prestige, whereas wealthy nations often connect prestige and power with thinness.

Despite the profits, however, the success rate for these programs and their products is less than perfect. For various reasons, diets don't work for everyone. As a result, many individuals long for the magic pill that will melt their pounds away—and pharmaceutical companies have spent vast sums of money developing drugs to address the issue. Surgical treatments are also available to treat people at great risk of health complications as a result of their obesity.

But What Is Obesity?

As is the case with many medical conditions, obesity has a medical definition based on research. Doctors need these definitions in order to decide which treatments are appropriate; diagnosis usually requires an exact definition of the problem.

Among the methods doctors commonly use for diagnosing obesity is a calculation known as body mass index (BMI). For most people, this number serves as a good estimate of their total body fat. Much research has established a healthy ratio of body weight to height. The ratio is usually referred to as the BMI. The use of BMI allows doctors to assess the health of patients of all heights.

In terms of health, research has indicated that a healthy BMI ranges between 19 and 24, while a BMI between 30 and 34 is considered obese. Anything above 34 is thought to be *morbidly* obese and in great danger of health problems. The stress placed on internal organs rises as weight increases, and health problems begin as a result.

Although BMI is a useful for tool for assessing obesity, it has its drawbacks. The limitations of BMI are apparent when we consider that most athletes are not obese even though they are heavy. BMI calculations tend to overestimate the percentage of body fat in athletes, and underestimate the percentage in older people, who have lost muscle mass over the years.

Thankfully, doctors have other tools at their disposal they can use to assess the condition of a patient with a high BMI. Waist measurement, for example, tends to be a very good indicator of patient body mass. When the waist measurements are combined with BMI calculations, a very good picture of the health of the patient can be created. The National Institutes of Health (NIH) has published a chart com-

According to BMI calculations, more than 60 percent of the population are obese or overweight.

Determining Your Body Mass Index (BMI)

To use the table below, find the appropriate height in the left-hand column. Move across the row to the given weight. The number at the top of the column is the BMI for that height and weight.

BMI (kg/m^2)	19	20	21	22	23	24	25	26	27	28	29	30	35	40
Height (in.)	Weight (lb.)													
58	91	96	100	105	110	115	119	124	129	134	138	143	167	191
59	94	99	104	109	114	119	124	128	133	138	143	148	173	198
60	97	102	107	112	118	123	128	133	138	143	148	153	179	204
61	100	106	111	116	122	127	132	137	143	148	153	158	185	211
62	104	109	115	120	126	131	136	142	147	153	158	164	191	218
63	107	113	118	124	130	135	141	146	152	158	163	169	197	225
64	110	116	122	128	134	140	145	151	157	163	169	174	204	232
65	114	120	126	132	138	144	150	156	162	168	174	180	210	240
66	118	124	130	136	142	148	155	161	167	173	179	186	216	247
67	121	127	134	140	146	153	159	166	172	178	185	191	223	255
68	125	131	138	144	151	158	164	171	177	184	190	197	230	262
69	128	135	142	149	155	162	169	176	182	189	196	203	236	270
70	132	139	146	153	160	167	174	181	188	195	202	207	243	278
71	136	143	150	157	165	172	179	186	193	200	208	215	250	286
72	140	147	154	162	169	177	184	191	199	206	213	221	258	294
73	144	151	159	166	174	182	189	197	204	212	219	227	265	302
74	148	155	163	171	179	186	194	202	210	218	225	233	272	311
75	152	160	168	176	184	192	200	208	216	224	232	240	279	319
76	156	164	172	180	189	197	205	213	221	230	238	246	287	328

Body weight in pounds according to height and body mass index.

Risk of Associated Disease According to BMI and Waist Size			
BMI		Waist less than or equal to 40 in. (men) or 35 in. (women)	Waist greater than 40 in. (men) or 35 in. (women)
18.5 or less	Underweight	--	N/A
18.5 – 24.9	Normal	--	N/A
25.0 – 29.9	Overweight	Increased	High
30.0 – 34.9	Obese	High	Very High
35.0 – 39.9	Obese	Very High	Very High
40 or greater	Extremely Obese	Extremely High	Extremely High

bining the information from both BMI and waist measurement. According to the NIH chart, a man with a waist greater than 40 inches or a woman with a waist measurement of greater than 35 and with a BMI of 25 and greater is at increased risk of health problems. The risk increases with increasing BMI.

Another method of assessing body fat is a simple determination of the percentage of weight a person carries in body fat compared to total weight. For example, a person weighing 180 pounds with 18 pounds of body fat has approximately 10 percent body fat, which is not a bad percentage to have.

Several ways are used to determine the percentage of body fat on a body. The method most commonly used is a skin-fold measurement. A special set of calipers (like tongs) measure the width of a skin fold at specific positions. The measurements are averaged, and the resulting numbers are used to calculate body fat percentage.

Scales that determine body fat percentages by measuring an electrical current are available for purchase at department stores or pharmacies. The amount of fat can be determined by running a very small electrical current through the person's body from one metal pad to another, usually from one foot to the other. The ease with which the current passes through the body indicates the amount of fat present. The more fat a person

has, the harder it is for the current to pass through the body. These are the bioelectrical impedance analysis (BIA) scales.

Hydrostatic weighing is another less commonly used method for determining body fat percentage. First, the individual is weighed when dry. The next step requires that the person be submerged in water up to the neck and breathe out all the air he can. The water is weighed, and the percentage of fat in the person's body can be determined relatively accurately. This particular method is rare compared to other methods because the equipment is very specialized and expensive, and some people are uncomfortable in the water. Doctors can also use a method known as DEXA, which scans the patient's body with X rays and determines the amount of body fat with high accuracy. The procedure is very expensive and therefore used only infrequently. Each scan costs more than a hundred dollars, so most insurance companies won't cover its use. However, DEXA is the most accurate of all the methods for determining the percentage of body fat.

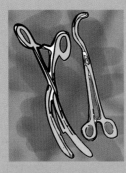

Why Do We Worry About Obesity So Much?

The NIH classified obesity as a chronic disease for many reasons. More than one-quarter of the population of the United States qualifies as obese, and at least three hundred thousand deaths can be associated with it each year. Obesity ranks as the second-leading cause of preventable death in the country. According to a recent study by the RAND organization, obesity is more damaging to a person's health than smoking or excess alcohol consumption.

Obesity adversely affects most of the internal organs of the human body. Fat can build up in the spaces between the organs, or within them, changing

An estimated 70 percent of all cases of heart disease are linked to obesity.

how efficiently they work. Fatty deposits can even build up in a person's brain over time. Another danger is that fat has a tendency to accumulate toxic substances such as mercury, which can have poisonous effects on the human body. The accumulation of toxins may also play a role in increased incidence of certain cancers in people who are obese.

Many additional health conditions are tied to obesity. For example, people with severe weight problems have higher instances of arthritis because the fatty tissue builds up in their joints, causing pain and reducing the ability to bend or move around the joint. Carpal tunnel syndrome, a painful wrist condition, is four times more likely to affect obese individuals. Pregnant women should be aware that obesity can increase the risk of some potentially deadly birth defects in their child. High blood pressure and

cardiovascular disease are also associated with obesity, and increase with increasing body fat.

One of the most common diseases that affect obese people is type 2 diabetes, which results in blood sugar levels that are dangerously high. More than 90 percent of all people with this disorder are overweight. Many researchers have found that obesity is the single most important factor leading to the development of this disease.

Anyone who smokes is obviously at risk for health complications, but the danger is much greater when combined with obesity. Smoking alone greatly increases a person's risk of cancer and heart disease, but when combined with obesity, the risk of contracting either of these potentially deadly diseases is nearly four times more likely.

Clearly, obesity is dangerous to the individual affected. The costs to society as a whole should be considered as well. As the second most common cause of death, obesity is a very real public concern. The annual cost of treating obesity throughout the country exceeds $102 billion per year, more than 12 percent of the United States' annual health care budget. This is a considerable amount of money spent on a single health problem, but keep in mind, obesity is a very common problem. Dollars spent preventing and treating obesity is in truth not much different than those spent searching for a cure for cancer. A disease is a disease, regardless of the causes.

What Are the Treatment Options?

Many people assume that losing weight is simply a matter of willpower; they think that with enough self-discipline, a person's fat will simply melt away. Obesity, however, is a medical condition. Some people simply cannot control their own weight, and the reasons for this can be varied; genetic and environmental factors come into play. When this is the case, medical treatment may be the only option that will work. Patient health is the goal of all medical professionals, and the burden on doctors is to find a way to bring a patient's weight under control and to a healthy level.

Obviously, however, the focus cannot be solely on the doctors to find a solution to the problem. The patient must also bear some of the burden. Thankfully, scientists have been producing a large amount of research in the area, and many nonmedical, highly effective options have been developed in recent years.

One of the most obvious strategies for reducing weight is to limit the amount of food we eat. Eat less; weigh less. Of course, this is often easier said than done. Restaurants across the country serve portions that are far beyond the size necessary to maintain a healthy level of major nutrients. The public has grown to expect huge portions of food, and many people express anger when this is not the case. The trouble comes from having the extra food available. Many people will eat every last scrap of food on their plate at a meal, regardless of the amount of food they started with. Parents who tell their children to clean their plates because of starving children in other parts of the world may not be doing their offspring any favors.

A simple increase in physical activity each day can also have a huge effect on the weight of a person. Move more; weigh less. By burning a hundred more calories each day, a person can lose up to ten pounds each year. Something as simple as walking up the stairs rather than taking the elevator

In order for a person to gain a pound, they must eat 3,500 calories and get no additional exercise.

can make a big difference. Of course, this strategy is also very hard for many people. Many obese people are self-conscious about participating in exercise activities in public places, and exercising at home can be hard to maintain.

Often, obese people will try a handful of commercially available dieting products, such as the Atkins Diet or Weight-Watchers, before seeking professional medical treatment. All too often, the weight lost while using these diets and products returns soon after stopping usage. When dieting fails, doctors have a handful of options for the medical treatment of obesity. Some are long-term approaches that change the way a person eats for the rest of her life, while others are short term, to be used for a few months at most.

Medical treatments for obesity can be grouped into one of two categories: drug therapy (discussed further in chapters 2 through 5) or surgery

(discussed in chapters 6 through 8). Each is a relatively drastic option, reserved for people deemed at risk of immediate danger due to their condition. According to the American Obesity Association (AOA), these treatments are only available to people whose BMI exceeds 30. Some people having other risk factors, such as high blood pressure, are eligible with a lower BMI.

The United States Food and Drug Administration (FDA), the agency responsible for determining whether a new drug is safe for use in humans, must give its official approval before a medication can be marketed or sold in the United States. The process for clearing a drug before patient use is long and expensive, and very few drug therapies have been approved for long-term use. Only two medications have been approved for use longer than one year: sibutramine, which is marketed as Meridia®; and orlistat, marketed as Xenical®.

Drug companies use two names for their products: the trade name and the chemical name. This serves to identify the brand name drug from any generic drugs that may enter the market.

Many drugs have been approved for short-term usage. Any usage that exceeds more than a few weeks or months is considered long term, though it is not uncommon for people to misuse the drugs by taking them for more than the approved length of time. To ignore the FDA guidelines for a drug's usage can be very dangerous and sometimes results in severe complications for the patient. Some people have also found that they lose weight rapidly by combining two or more of the drugs. The widespread use of a therapy commonly called Fen-Phen, a name taken from the combined names of the two drugs involved, had disastrous results for some people. For them, the combination of the two drugs caused severe damage to their heart valves, resulting in reports of pulmonary hypertension and even some deaths.

Surgery may seem drastic, but the health issues associated with obesity can be deadly. Immediate and long-lasting treatments can sometimes be the difference between life and death. Among the procedures commonly used to reduce a patient's weight are four true treatments in two categories and two cosmetic ones. A few other treatments exist that are not often used because they are too restrictive to the patient.

Roux-en-Y gastric bypass surgery and biliopancreatic diversion are true treatments that result in a change in the routing of the digestive system. An

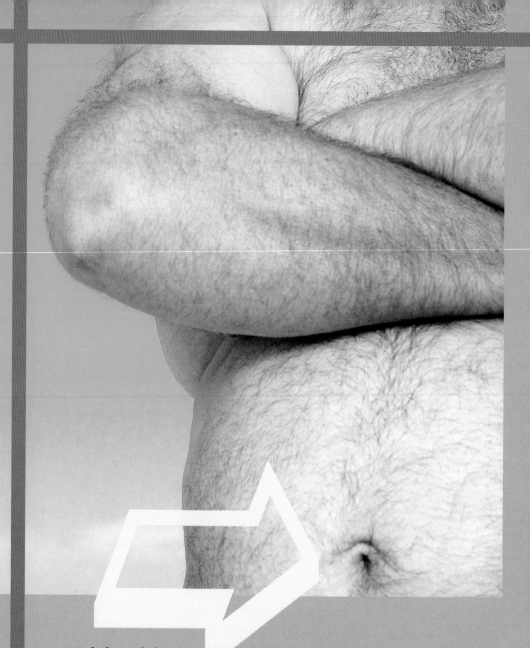

actual physical change to the digestive system greatly reduces the effectiveness of the system to take in nutrients from food, causing a decrease in the
number of calories a person can absorb from each piece of food that he eats.
The result is usually a relatively rapid weight loss that lasts for a many years,
if not a lifetime.

Adjustable gastric banding and vertical gastric banding are also true treatments. By reducing the size of the usable area of the stomach, weight can be controlled effectively for a long period of time, perhaps for life.

Liposuction is another method used by many who have uncontrolled weight. Sucking the fat cells from trouble areas is a temporary fix and is mainly cosmetic, but the change is immediate and visible. Liposuction cannot be considered a true treatment because it does not affect weight on a long-term basis. In addition, the tummy tuck, known to doctors as abdominoplasty, is a short-term treatment that does not offer any real long-term benefits.

In the past, doctors, recognizing the importance of patient weight, have gone as far as to wire shut the jaws of the individual. Obviously, this is a very severe way to deal with the issue, and the method is seldom used today because it restricts the patient in many ways other than eating. The results of any drastic treatments should always improve the patient's quality of life, so most doctors now frown on this particular treatment.

Some people, however, are so desperate to reduce their weight that they are willing to take extreme measures. Some may even takes steps that actually endanger their health. For instance, a teenage girl bought a pill through the Internet that promised to reduce weight. The pill was amazingly effective—and no wonder: it contained tapeworm eggs!

Our culture is often *prejudiced* against people who are obese. Sometimes overweight people are thought to be less attractive, lazy, lacking in self-discipline, or less intelligent. This social stigma can contribute to an individual's willingness to take extreme steps to tackle his obesity.

In reality, however, the percentage of body fat a person carries has nothing to do with her value as a human being. Obesity is a medical condition, accompanied by significant health risks. As we further explore some of the more extreme treatment options, keep in mind these are medical treatments appropriate only for the most serious conditions. They are never quick-fix methods for complying with a culture obsessed with thinness.

Obesity and Self-Esteem

Christina walked down the hall at school without speaking to anyone at all. Her head was down, and her face burned with shame. Other kids around her gathered books from their lockers, talking and laughing with their friends. Each peal of laughter made Christina cringe. She didn't hear the jokes the other kids told before the laughter started, so she thought each laugh was aimed at her.

Christina didn't have funny clothes or an odd hairstyle, and she wasn't ugly. She knew her clothes were fine, her hair looked nice, and her face was attractive. But Christina truly believed every laugh was directed at her because she was overweight. She was so convinced that everyone was laughing at her that she didn't realize no one was even looking at her, let alone laughing at her at all.

Christina's mother was overweight as well, and Christina grew up watching her mother try and fail with a string of diets, constantly complaining about her weight to anyone who would listen. When Christina was getting ready for her first day of kindergarten, she had asked her mother if her new dress made her look fat. She tried her first diet when she was eight; she couldn't count the number of diets she had tried since then. Every month the magazines at the supermarket promised her they had the answer to her weight problem—and Christina tried them all. But for some reason, she never lost more than a few pounds; what she did lose, she quickly regained. She got books out of the library about weight loss and read all sorts of warnings about the risks of being over-weight, but she just couldn't seem to get it under con-trol. Instead, as she went through her teens, every year her weight crept a little higher.

When the school nurse suggested to Christina that she consult a doctor, Christina felt a huge sense of relief. She was tired of hating herself. She knew she'd never fit in at school—but she didn't know what to do. The more depressed she felt, the more she wanted to eat. No matter how hard she tried, the answer didn't seem to lie inside herself. But if she had a medical problem, something a doctor could help her tackle, then maybe she wasn't such a bad person after all.

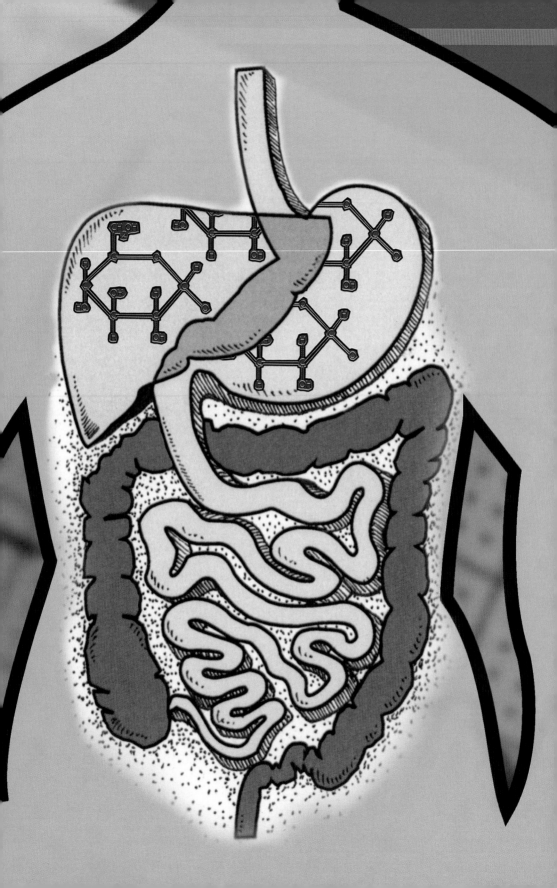

Chapter 2

Isn't There Anything to Keep Me From Being So Hungry All the Time?

- How Your Body Tells You When You're Hungry

- How Medications Can Reduce Your Hunger

What makes you eat? The most obvious answer is this: you eat because you're hungry. Unfortunately, the sensation we label as "hunger" is not always related to our bodies' actual need for food. Emotional, environmental, and physiological circumstances may trigger our bodies' hunger responses, even when we don't really need more food.

One of the most obvious classes of drugs used to treat obesity is the type that reduces hunger. A decrease in the amount of food eaten has an immediate effect on the weight of an individual.

How Your Body Tells You When You're Hungry

For the most part, chemical substances within the body control hunger. The body produces them in response to the cues such as the amount of sugar in the bloodstream. Some people lack the chemicals that control the feelings of hunger and fullness normally felt throughout the day by most other people

Serotonin, a chemical released by glands around the brain, is found in the stomach, small intestine, and bloodstream. Throughout the day, the glands produce serotonin, using up vitamins and minerals in the process. When there is a lack of the necessary nutrients, serotonin levels in the body drop, stimulating a feeling of hunger.

Catecholamines are a class of *hormones* that are thought to affect hunger. Blood-sugar levels rise and fall as a normal consequence of our daily eating schedules, and when the levels fall below a certain point, a specific catecholamine that's tied to hunger, noradrenaline, drops as well, triggering a hunger message that the body sends to your brain.

How Medications Can Reduce Your Hunger

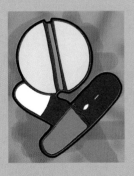

Most of the drugs that work by reducing hunger take advantage of blood chemistry to change the hunger patterns of the patient. The FDA, however, has only approved one medication for long-term use (more than one year) that acts by reducing how hungry we feel. Called sibutramine, it is sold under the brand name Meridia. By increasing the amount of noradrenaline, serotonin, and *dopamine* in the brain, the drug reduces feelings

A Candidate for Appetite-Control Medication

The group of guys sitting in the back row of study hall stifled their laughter so as not to attract the teacher's attention. They could hardly keep their voices under control. Joe kept them in stitches every day. They didn't always get that much work done, but they had a ton of fun.

Joe was the funniest guy in the senior class. He had been voted the most-likely-to-succeed class member, the best-dressed student, the most talkative senior, and on and on. He won the race for "Class Clown" hands down, and his picture would appear in the yearbook holding a rubber chicken and a whoopee cushion.

Joe wasn't an athlete, but he managed to be one of the most popular kids anyway. He was always laughing and so was anyone else who was near him—but he had one private sadness: he couldn't seem to keep his weight under control. He sometimes thought that the reason he was funny was because he was working so hard to make sure everyone was laughing *with* him and not *at* him.

Joe's doctor was worried about Joe because he couldn't walk up stairs without getting out of breath, and he avoided any physical activity for fear of looking silly. He had tried to eat healthier, but he had only lost five pounds, which didn't even make a difference in his pants size. Dr. Thompson suggested that they talk about some other alternatives. She told Joe she could prescribe some medicine that would help him feel less hungry and eat smaller portions. Taking the medicine had a few risks, but the doctor thought those risks were balanced by the risks of being obese.

Joe started taking his new medicine right away. He didn't tell any of his friends about it, but he couldn't wait to see if it would work. It was worth a try!

of hunger in patients. Meridia was approved in 1997 and has been successfully used by thousands of people to reduce their weight. Usually, once the patient loses the desired amount of weight, he stops taking the medication. Sometimes, however, this results in the regaining of much of the weight that was lost. Since it is approved for long-term use, Meridia can be prescribed and used for many years, preventing the return of pounds shed through using this treatment method.

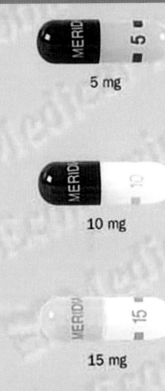

5 mg

10 mg

15 mg

Clinical studies have shown that Meridia is also very effective in short-term weight-loss situations. When a group of overweight women were studied for an eight-week period, each woman consumed the same number of calories per day, and half of them were given Meridia. The women given the drug lost much more weight than those who did not receive it, indicating that the drug is an effective weight-loss tool.

As with other weight-loss drugs, Meridia is prescribed only to individuals thought to be in danger because of their weight. A person with a BMI of greater than 30, or 27 if they have other risk factors such as high blood pressure, is a candidate to receive this treatment. The treatment works best when combined with healthy eating habits and an increase in exercise.

Meridia is not problem free, however. It has some potentially dangerous side effects. Some patients have experienced high blood pressure, and it is not safe for those with heart or kidney disease. Meridia is not well studied in pregnant women, so doctors recommend that drug treatment stop if a woman knows she is carrying a child. Sleeplessness, dry mouth, and upset stomach are some of the more common side effects of taking Meridia. These side effects, however, are far less unpleasant than the effects of untreated obesity. Some patients, however, have more severe side effects, such as chest pain and shortness of breath, which must be dealt with on an individual basis.

A combination therapy called Fen-Phen, which combined Phentermine with Fenfluramine, was quite effective in reducing weight in the people taking it, but it had the unfortunate potential side effect of causing heart valve malfunction, sometimes leading to death. The FDA approved the two drugs for individual use in the 1970s, and in 1994, doctors, sometimes in conjunction with weight-loss businesses, began prescribing the Fen-Phen combination as a weight-loss treatment based on a single study. More than 18 million prescriptions were written by the end of 1996, even though this was not the FDA-approved use of the drugs. The FDA quickly banned it because of the frequency of the deadly side effects. Nearly one-third of the patients developed heart valve defects, and many died. Some people continued to buy Fen-Phen on the black market, even after they became aware of the serious risks. These people were so desperate to be thin that they were willing to risk serious health problems, even death, to achieve their goal.

In response to heavy pressure by the FDA, Fenfluramine was pulled from the market. Phentermine remains available for prescription use because substantial research indicates it is safe if used according to the FDA guidelines. Many patients lose weight successfully while being treated and have good long-term outcomes.

Phentermine works in much the same way as Meridia. The brain responds to Phentermine with an increase in blood pressure and heart rate, and a decrease in appetite. The therapy is also more effective when combined with exercise and a healthy diet, a common theme among drug treatments for weight loss.

One potential side effect of Phentermine treatment is addiction. The drug is very closely related to amphetamines, which are commonly abused illegal drugs. Phentermine affects the nervous system so strongly that the patient

can become psychologically and physically addicted after just a few treatments. The drug is not for long-term use and should be taken only for eight to twelve weeks at a time. Some of the more common side effects include nausea, chest pain, and difficulty breathing, none of which should be ignored.

In the United States, for example, between 35 and 40 percent of women are attempting to lose weight at any given time. (Among men, the percentages are lower: between 20 and 25 percent.) Obesity is such a costly and controversial issue in the country that many health insurance providers will not offer coverage for it. Nevertheless, many people are so desperate to lose weight that they are willing to pay for expensive drug therapies out-of-pocket.

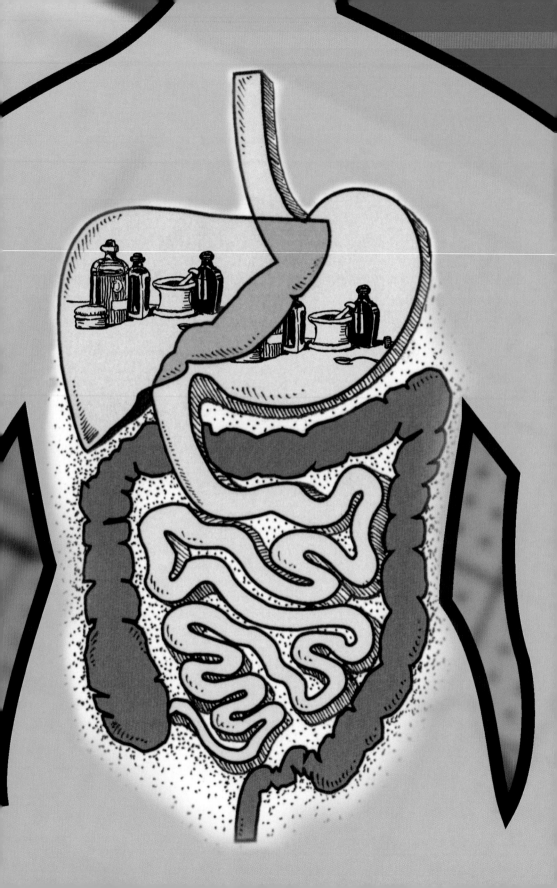

Chapter 3

Is There Any~~thing~~ That Chan~~ges~~ How My Body Deals with Fat?

- The Process of Digestion

- Xenical

- A Vital Stop-Gap Measure

The Process of Digestion

The human body has a very specific way of digesting and absorbing fats. Each organ of the digestive system is specialized to deal with one or possibly two nutrient types. The entire system works together to absorb as much energy as possible from each bit of food.

For example, sugary foods are digested mainly in the mouth and stomach. Sugars dissolve relatively easily and are quickly absorbed into the bloodstream. An *enzyme* known as salivary amylase does most of the work in the digestion of sugars. Proteins, on the other hand, are digested primarily in the stomach by the enzyme pepsin and by powerful hydrochloric acid. Fats are mainly absorbed in the small intestine, where the enzyme lipase breaks them down. These mechanisms provide pharmaceutical companies with some very appealing targets for drug therapies to address the obesity problem. By blocking or limiting the action of these enzymes, the amount of nutrients taken in by the body from a given piece of food can be decreased.

Xenical

Like Meridia, Xenical® is the only drug of this sort that has been FDA approved. Xenical prevents fat from being processed and absorbed by the body in the small intestine, allowing it to pass through the body like a waste product. Since fat contains so much stored energy, prevention of fat absorption greatly reduces the number of calories in a piece of food.

Xenical is one of the most-tested weight-loss drugs on the market today. More than 30,000 patients participated in clinical trials during 2002. Since its approval in 1998, over 13 million patients worldwide have taken the drug. Most of the results have been positive, with most of the people taking it reporting weight loss and improved health. The thing that sets Xenical apart is that it seems to be an effective tool for weight management. Patients were able to lose weight and keep it off for long periods of time.

In one well-documented study, researchers tested the effectiveness of Xenical in weight loss and maintenance. A group of 430 men and women with BMIs between 30 and 43 were given Xenical, and their weight was monitored for one year. More than 70 percent of the patients experienced rapid weight loss and were able to maintain the loss for more than six months. More than 50 percent of the patients lost 10 percent of their total body weight and kept the weight off over the course of the study. All of the patients were examined regularly by doctors and found to have made healthy reductions in blood pressure and resting heart rate.

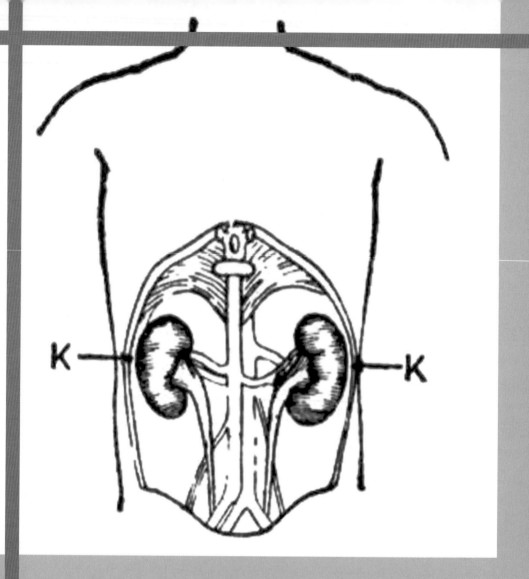

When a piece of fatty food enters the small intestine, it mixes with several enzymes, including lipase, and it slowly dissolves. The products of this process are absorbed by the blood vessels in the walls of the intestine and spread throughout the body for fuel. Xenical works by stopping the action of the lipase, preventing the breakdown of the fats in the food. The fat is excreted undigested, and the calories it contains are not absorbed. When combined with a decreased-calorie diet, Xenical is a very effective weight-control medicine.

An Interesting Side Effect

Studies have indicated that Xenical might help to slow or prevent the growth of certain cancers, including prostate cancer. Some cancers may need an enzyme that is closely related to lipase in order to grow. Xenical appears to interfere with the activity of this enzyme as well, effectively preventing the cancer from growing.

Further clinical studies are required before the real effectiveness of Xenical in treating cancers can be determined, but it is a promising lead in a very important area of medicine.

Unfortunately, Xenical can have some unpleasant effects on the individual taking it. For example, the fat being excreted causes runny, oily, and gassy stool. At times, patients find that they have sudden, uncontrollable diarrhea. In addition, many vitamins the body needs are fat soluable. People taking Xenical are usually required to take a multivitamin to supplement their normal dietary intake to make up for the loss in vitamins.

People who have had prior problems with their kidneys or gallbladder should not take Xenical, because good kidney and gallbladder function is required to keep the medication from building up in their blood. Pregnant women are also discouraged from taking the drug to prevent any birth defects it may cause. Xenical can also have an effect on blood sugar because

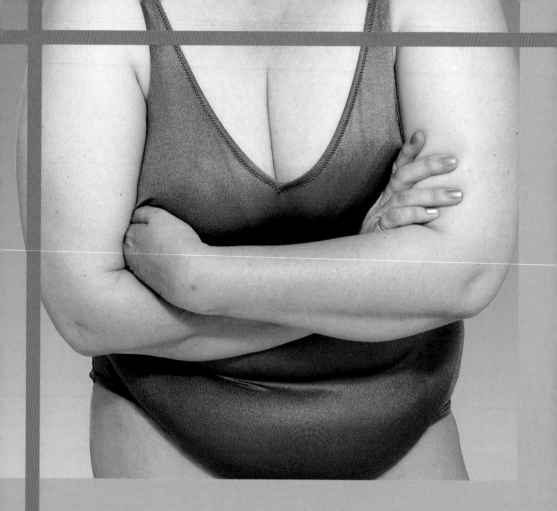

some of the by-products of fat digestion are sugars. **Diabetics** need to be aware of this fact before they start taking the drug.

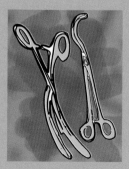

A Vital Stop-Gap Measure

On average, adults consume a diet that consists of about 12 percent saturated fat. Fast-food restaurants and many snack foods are high in fat, and our on-the-go lifestyle encourages us to depend on these quick and often unhealthy foods. We may not realize the full price we pay for these eating habits.

Saturated fat has been implicated in many health problems, including heart and cardiovascular disease. Obesity more than doubles a person's risk of developing high blood pressure, which affects about 26 percent of obese men and women. The yearly cost of obesity-related high blood pressure is nearly $1.5 billion. Nearly half of all cases of breast cancer are diagnosed in obese women, and approximately 42 percent of colon cancer cases are diagnosed among obese individuals.

Clearly, the costs of our eating habits are enormous, both to individuals and to society as a whole. Ultimately, the best solution is to change our lifestyle—but this will not be fast or easy to accomplish. In the meantime, many obese individuals face serious risks.

Medications that block fat absorption are not the answer to our society's unhealthy lifestyle. But these medications can provide hope to individuals who desperately need to lose weight in order to protect their health.

Obesity's Health Risks

Jessica sat at the dinner table with her head in hands, not taking part in the family conversation. Her mom watched her from across the table; after a moment, she asked, "Jess, you don't have another one of those headaches, do you?"

Jess shook her head. Her mother had told her she would take her to the doctor if the headaches didn't stop, and Jess hated going to the doctor. Her mother kept staring at her, though, and finally, Jess gave in and admitted that the headache was worse than ever.

A few days later, Jess sat next to her mother in Dr. Chen's waiting room. When the nurse called her name, she managed to make it through her least favorite part (stepping on the scale!) and then held out her arm for the blood pressure cuff. Jess could tell by the nurse's face she wasn't happy with the numbers.

Dr. Chen had been Jess's doctor since she was three years old. Jess might hate going to the doctor's, but she didn't hate Dr. Chen. He was a small man and always very smiley. When he opened the door this time, however, he had a grave look on his face. He asked her if she minded if he called in her mom to hear what he had to say.

Jess shrugged, and Dr. Chen came back with Jess's mom. They all sat down together, and Dr. Chen began to talk. "Jess, your blood pressure is really high. If we don't get it down, even though you're only seventeen, you could be at risk of having a stroke, a heart attack, or other really serious problems. I want you to start on medication for your blood pressure right away, but I also think we need to address something else. You have no family history of high blood pressure, so I think that it might be so high because you are overweight."

Jess flushed. She knew she was heavy, but she hated to hear anyone say it.

Dr. Chen continued, "I think there might be something we can do to help you. I know diets haven't worked for you, so I want you to try taking some medicine. This medicine will keep your stomach from taking in all the fat in the food you eat. It has some pretty unpleasant side effects if you eat too much, but it shouldn't be too bad if you make good food choices. I think we can help you lose a lot of weight and maybe even be able to take you off the blood pressure medication. Are you game?"

Jess smiled through her embarrassment and nodded.

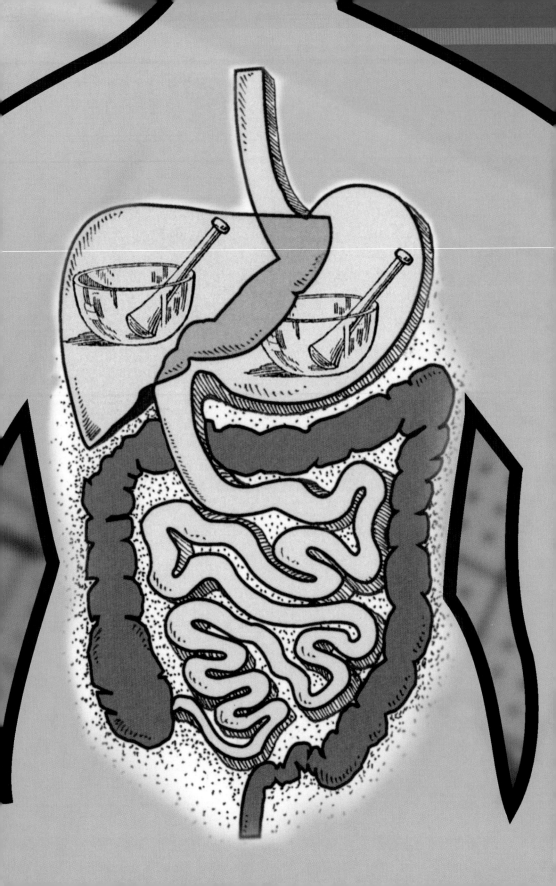

Chapter 4

Is There Anything I Can Use to Help Me Lose Weight Without Going to the Doctor?

- Risky Business
- The "Natural" Way
- Ephedrine
- St. John's Wort
- Pyruvate
- Aloe
- Dandelion
- Guarana
- Guar Gum
- Natural Diuretics

Risky Business

As Eric walked down the aisle of weight-loss products at Wal-Mart, a heavy woman pushing a shopping cart filled with snacks and soda walked by him, looking at the bottles of herbal supplements spread out before her. She smiled at Eric and picked up a few bottles from the shelves.

"These are the ones I use. I tried a couple of them, but they didn't do much for me. Then I lost six pounds when I started taking all three together a few days ago. You should try them." She pointed to the three products she had just picked up.

Eric was one of the biggest players on the football team. He had a competitive fire burning in him, and he was always looking for anything that would

give him an edge. If he could just lose a few pounds, he might be able to break all the school records for a running back.

"Thanks," he told the woman. He knew he needed to lose weight, but he didn't like the idea of dieting, and he sure didn't want to talk to his doctor about it. This could be exactly what he needed. He gathered up a few of the remedies without really bothering to read the labels.

As soon as Eric got home, he opened up the bottles and took the dose the label said he should. He thought how happy he would be if the pills had the same effect the woman had experienced. Then he would finally be able to get rid of those extra pounds that were slowing him down on the football field.

The following morning, at football practice, Eric collapsed. The coach began CPR immediately and worked until the ambulance arrived to take Eric to the hospital.

Doctors had to work hard to save his life, but Eric was lucky. He had taken a combination of pills that caused his heart to stop beating when he exercised. He lived—but he was never able to play football again.

Many over-the-counter weight-loss treatments are supposed to help a person lose weight. Most of these are not FDA tested or approved, and should be taken with extreme care. Some are harmless but worthless, while others have the desired effect but, because of the lack of research supporting their safety, the FDA has not issued its approval.

The "Natural" Way

Many over-the-counter treatments are herbal supplements popularized by the recent trend toward all things "natural." In a grocery or department store, a shopper can buy a vast array of different herbal supplements, all reported to have some healing property or nutritional value. Ginseng, echinacea, ginger root,

flaxseed oil, lavender oil, and shark cartilage are all examples of the sorts of things one can find, each with a different function that supposedly makes life better.

Herbal remedies are not necessarily bad. Research indicates that many are effective health aids. The problem with over-the-counter remedies is that they are not thoroughly tested. The manufacturers rely on word-of–mouth—and infomercials on television—to sell their products, and they don't wish to pay the large amounts of money required to pass the rigorous FDA-testing procedures. Although this keeps prices down for consumers—it also allows manufacturers to get rich quick, without complying with FDA regulations.

Lacking FDA approval allows the manufacturers to market their products as nondrugs, which largely frees them of the burden of having to provide information to the public about the real effectiveness of the product. Independent researchers have studied some of these products and shown to have some effect. Others have shown no effect at all (save to lighten the pocket of the consumer!).

Ephedrine

Until recently, ephedrine was the most popular weight-loss remedy sold over-the-counter. The FDA has in fact approved one form of ephedrine—ephedrine hydrochloride—but this is the only type of ephedrine that can be legally considered a drug, and this form is not found in weight-loss products. The most common form used in non-FDA–approved products is an *extract* from a plant found in the United States. A similar plant exists in China as well.

A *stimulant* that affects the nervous system, ephedrine has been used for decades as a component of nasal decongestants and asthma treatments. Ephedrine is also well known in athletic circles for its performance-enhancing properties. It causes high blood pressure and elevated heart rate, and is believed to increase the *metabolism* of those taking it for extended periods of time. This gives athletes more energy and allows calories to be burned more quickly.

Ephedrine has been linked to several deaths. As a result, it has been banned until more research can be done. Ephedrine may

Ephedra (Ma Huang)

cause severe bleeding in the brain, as well as sudden heart attacks and strokes.

St. John's Wort

St. John's wort has become increasingly popular in herbal weight-loss supplements, though is better known as an over-the-counter treatment for depression. It is one of the ingredients of herbal Fen-Phen, reported by the manufacturer to be effective for weight loss. Few studies have verified this claim, so St. John's wort should be taken very carefully. Some scientists feel that it is only a matter of time before serious problems start to show up among people taking this supplement.

Pyruvate

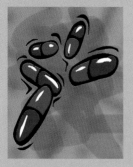

When the body breaks down sugars and proteins, a chemical known as pyruvate is produced. Some studies have indicated that pyruvate can have some effect in helping people lose weight, so herbal manufacturers have begun to offer it for sale. Few studies have been done to examine the claims that pyruvate boosts metabolism, promotes burning of body fat, and increases energy. Pyruvate does appear to be safe, as it is found naturally in many foods, including red wine, cheese, and apples. Appearances can be misleading, though, so care is advised in taking this supplement.

Aloe

Perhaps one of the most surprising weight-loss supplements recently produced is aloe. Long used as a wound treatment, it was discovered that aloe causes a strong and urgent need to defecate. Aloe is often marketed as an internal cleanser. Supplements that cause reactions like this are not likely to be safe to take internally, as diarrhea is a warning sign of some potentially dangerous conditions. No proof has been offered that aloe is useful in keeping off weight.

Dandelion

Dandelion—yes, those fuzzy yellow flowers that dot the lawn—has also recently entered the market as a weight-loss supplement. A natural diuretic, dandelion causes frequent urination and can reduce the water weight a person carries. Many people are allergic to this supplement, and it can cause severe *dehydration* in long-term users. Some research has shown that dandelion may be carcinogenic, causing cancers in laboratory rats.

Guarana

In Brazil, native people have long known that the seeds of a certain plant have a stimulating effect when eaten or ground up and mixed with water or tea. Today, guarana is common in herbal remedy sections, as it speeds up metabolism and promotes frequent urination. One of the components of guarana extract is caffeine, which is known to cause high blood pressure. Guarana often interacts with medicines and can cause deadly complications in certain cases. The extract has some relatively powerful anti-clotting properties and can cause unstoppable bleeding in long-term users.

Guar Gum

The Indian cluster bean is the source of yet another powerful herbal extract. Guar gum is a type of dietary fiber, often used as a thickening substance in cooking or in medications. The action of guar gum is like a sponge; it absorbs water rapidly and swells up to twenty times its original size in the process. Some people who have used this substance to curb their appetites have had very dangerous intestinal blockages, requiring surgery to remove. Guar gum also causes rapid blood sugar changes, so diabetics must take extreme care in taking it.

Natural Diuretics

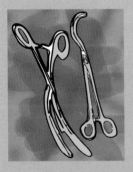

Many over-the-counter remedies contain natural *diuretics* that have been implicated in severe health problems. People should not take any weight-loss supplement that contains juniper seeds, which can cause kidney damage. Equistine and horse tail or shave grass have been found to cause brain damage or severe *convulsions*. For the most part, these supplements are not dangerous by themselves, but when taken in conjunction with medications they can have deadly interactions.

Losing weight is important for obese individuals, but the risks of taking unstudied herbal remedies are often not worth the gain. The majority of the gains made by taking an herbal supplement are usually temporary, especially in the case of diuretics. Most of the time, the weight comes right back after the person stops taking the supplement. The dangers of taking untested herbal supplements are not always readily apparent, but taking time to read the labels and research the individual ingredients can be a smart first step.

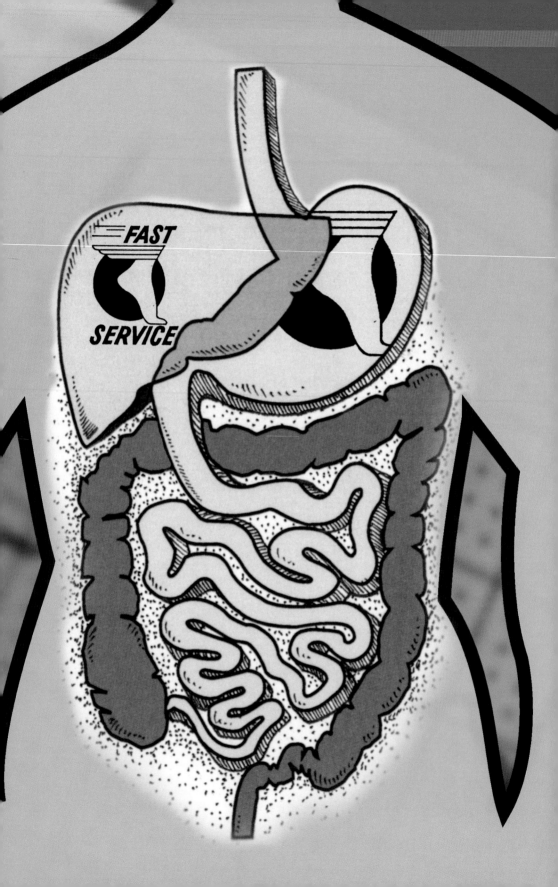

Chapter 5

What About the Chemicals My Body Already Makes?

- The Body's Messengers

- Leptin and NPY

- CKK

- Melanocortins

- Glucagon

Tammy tried diet after diet, and even took prescription medication to help her lose weight. The drugs worked, but soon after she stopped taking the medicine, she gained the weight back.

She did everything the doctor asked her to: increased her exercise, decreased the amount of food she ate, and changed the types of foods she ate. She knew her doctor was worried about her health because of the stress her weight put on her heart and other internal organs. She certainly wanted to live a long, healthy life.

Her doctor informed her that she might have another option: hormone therapy. This confused Tammy. She thought hormone therapy was only for older women who were going through *menopause*.

Her doctor explained, "There are chemical messengers responsible for many functions in our bodies. Many of them are involved in keeping weight at a healthy level. Your body might have a shortage of a very important hormone. We are going to run some tests to find out, if that's okay with you."

The prospect of finally finding an answer excited Tammy. She agreed to let the doctor draw some blood for testing. She did not understand how the test worked, and she did not really care. All she wanted was to know whether she could finally get some control over her weight.

"Well, Tammy," her doctor told her several days later, "I think you may be pleased to hear we have finally found the reason for your struggles. It seems your body is lacking a very important hormone that sends messages telling your cells how to process sugars. The good news is that a pharmaceutical company has agreed to include you in a clinical trial for a new therapy that should increase the amount of the hormone in your blood."

The Body's Messengers

Hormones are chemicals produced by the cells of our bodies; they serve as messengers from one cell to another. Every internal organ produces and is affected by hormones. Our bodies produce numerous hormones with various functions. The action of hormones is widely varied, but most often, each hormone has a specific function and a specific target organ. Some change our mood; others affect our metabolism and feelings of hunger. Many are of interest to researchers and drug developers because they are key components in the process of weight gain and control.

Drug manufacturers are very interested in the concept of hormone therapy. The promise of using human hormones to treat health issues is appealing for many reasons. Hormones known to occur naturally in humans will have a reduced risk of dangerous interactions with other chemicals also found in the body. Unlike many chemical substances used in drugs, hormones are relatively common (since most people have them in abundance) and will be cheap to *mass produce*. A number of likely targets have been identified for the treatment of obesity, and each shows great promise.

Leptin and NPY

Leptin, for example, is a hormone produced in fatty tissues throughout the body. When people eat excess amounts of food, fat cells build up. Each fat cell produces leptin, increasing the overall amount of the hormone in the blood. Receptors in the brain monitor the amount of leptin in the blood as a way of regulat-

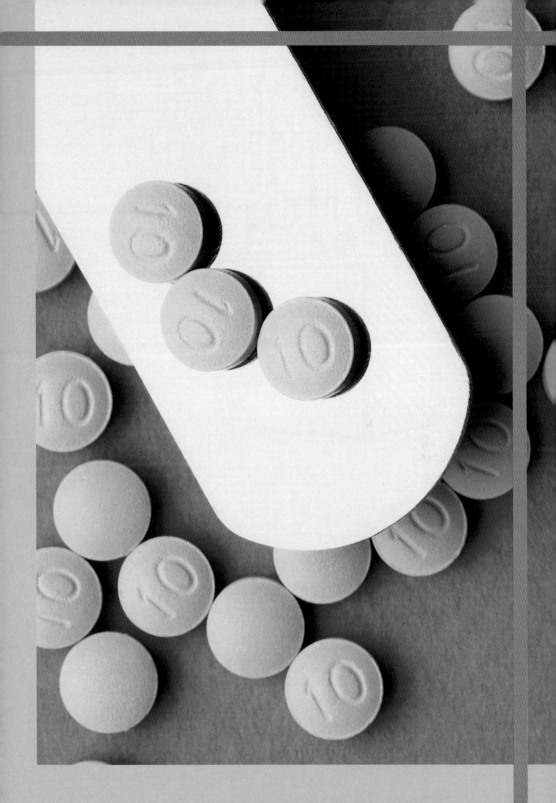

ing hunger and metabolism. When the brain detects high levels of leptin, hunger decreases. In addition, leptin inhibits the action of another hormone of interest, neuropeptide-Y (NPY), one of the chemicals associated with feelings of hunger.

Researchers feel that by giving an obese individual a dose of leptin on a regular basis, the patient will feel less hunger, since the individual may be experiencing a lack of leptin production in his fat cells. Many reasons exist for the deficiency, including diet and genetic causes. Hormone replacement therapy can bring the levels

There may be an increased risk of dangerous blood clotting in people taking large doses of leptin. Researchers have found that the incidence of blood clot-induced strokes was higher in people with high levels of leptin in their blood.

of leptin up to and beyond the normal level. Excess leptin, however, can cause too large of a decrease in appetite.

Some patients are less sensitive to leptin than others. In these cases, more leptin can be added to get the desired effect. Because leptin is a naturally occurring hormone, the negative effects of overloading the patient are minimal.

A study of mice injected with leptin indicates that therapy with the hormone can be very effective. Researchers documented a 30 percent weight loss in the mice over the course of two weeks. Each mouse ate less and exercised more throughout the course of the study.

NPY, the other hormone associated with leptin, is found around nerve cells. It is very important in stimulating feelings of hunger. Lab rats given large doses of this hormone became very hungry and ate large amounts of food. Over the course of several weeks, the formerly healthy rats became obese and sickly. The increase in NPY clearly caused the rats to overeat to the point of harming their health.

Treatments that limit the action of NPY will likely have an effect on the hunger of the patient. Doctors are eagerly waiting for the day that science finds a way to change the amount or effectiveness of NPY in a patient's bloodstream. Knowing that NPY is as important as it is, scientists can begin to look for ways to stop its action.

CKK

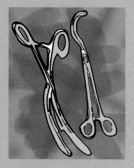

As we eat, the digestive process releases the nutrients in the food, which are then spread by the blood to all the cells of our bodies. In most people, the cells will release a critical hormone that informs their brains that they are full—they have enough nutrients for the time being. Cholecystokinin (CKK) is a hormone that stimulates the release of digestive enzymes and bile from the *gallblad-*

der. The brain interprets the presence of this chemical and reduces feelings of hunger.

Some people who **binge eat** are thought to either have defective CKK **receptors** or cells that are not producing enough of the hormone. In most cases, low levels of CKK seem to be the culprit, so hormone therapy could increase the amount of the chemical in the blood. Patients usually respond well to this treatment, reporting reduced hunger and subsequent weight loss.

A New Approach to Obesity Medication

In 2004, Merck & Co., the pharmaceutical giant, announced that it was working with Nastech Pharmaceutical Company to create a nasal spray that would help obese individuals lose weight. The spray is based on a hormone made by the intestines that travels through the bloodstream to the brain about 30 to 45 minutes after a person stops eating, telling the brain that the body has eaten enough. The nasal spray would allow the same chemical to move quickly through the nasal lining, into the bloodstream, and reach the brain within 20 to 35 minutes, convincing it that the body did not need to eat. Researchers predict the drug could reduce individuals' daily caloric intake by as much as 30 percent—which could translate into a 50-pound weight loss over a year.

Melanocortins

Other hormones found in the brain seem to play a very important role in controlling weight. The hypothalamus is a part of the brain that regulates many parts of our daily lives, from sleep to hunger. Melanocortins are a group of hormones that affect receptors on the hypothalamus. Like the other hormones previously discussed, melanocortins are present in the bloodstream of healthy people. The receptors on the hypothalamus detect the amount of melanocortins in the blood and we feel full in response.

Recent studies have shown that defects in the melanocortin receptors may be the cause of as much as five percent of all obesity in the United States alone. Researchers are developing treatments to modify the production and reception of melanocortins, but they are are having difficulties keeping the side effects to a minimum.

Glucagon

The pancreas produces glucagon, which controls the body's use and intake of carbohydrates. It also plays an important role in controlling food intake by limiting feelings of hunger in response to changes in blood sugar levels. Research has indicated that glucagon may be useful for weight loss because of its function in controlling blood sugar levels. Individuals who eat diets high in carbohydrates may find that they cannot control their weight. People whose diets are high in sugar have an increased production of insulin, a hormone that forces the glucose present in the food into the cells. In response, the cells change into fat cells, and the person experiences an increase in body fat. Glucagon prevents this by balancing insulin and changing the way the body stores and uses the nutrients.

Normally, glucagon is produced in response to protein digestion, but some people seem to be lacking the ability to produce enough of this hormone. The absence of glucagon can cause fat buildup in people. Replacing this naturally occurring hormone with injections of synthetic glucagon has led to a reduction in body fat among people participating in research. The challenge is finding a way to deliver the hormone long term and with few side effects.

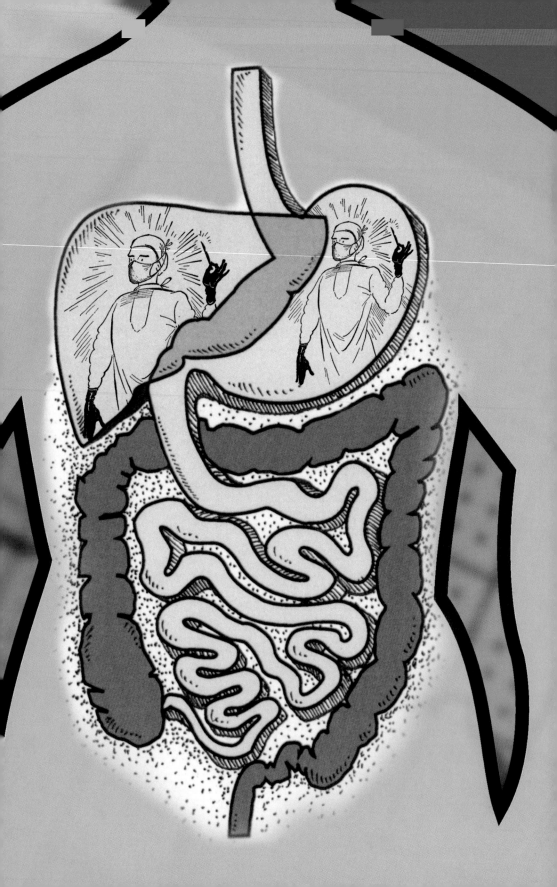

Chapter 6

What If the Medicine Isn't Right for Me?

- Drastic Steps

- Malabsorptive Surgeries

- Risks and Side Effects

- When Malabsorptive Surgeries Don't Work

Obviously, researchers have found many powerful pharmaceutical routes toward weight control. But these medications are not right for everyone. Some people experience dangerous side effects, while others may not respond to the drug in the desired way. Scientists continue to look for more and better medications. In the meantime, surgery offers another option for some individuals.

Drastic Steps

Going under the knife is never pleasant, but neither is being obese. The elevated risks associated with being obese are a greater danger to the patient than most of those associated with surgery. The percentage of people who suffer complications or death as a result of obesity is far greater than the percentage that suffers in association with the surgery.

People who cannot control their weight sometimes find that they must take what drastic steps to improve their health. Obesity is not a lifestyle choice; it is a disease. All treatments proven effective must be considered, even if they require surgery. The health risks of obesity are dangerous enough that every patient should keep trying until she is able to get her weight under control.

Bariatric surgery is another name for any surgical technique that is used to control weight.

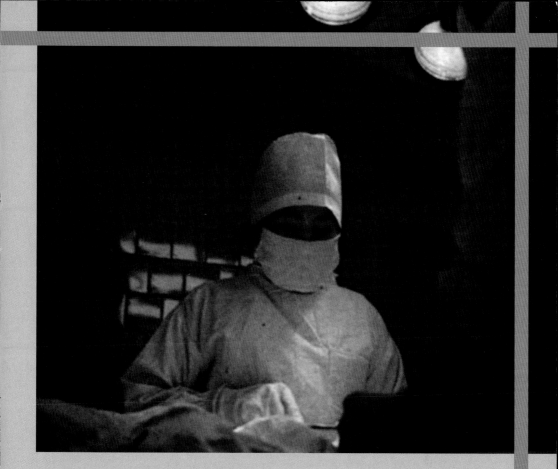

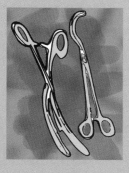

Malabsorptive Surgeries

Doctors have two surgical techniques at their disposal that actually change the pathway through the digestive system, thereby limiting the amount of food that gets processed and absorbed by the body. The term malabsorptive has been applied to them because they hinder the ability of the system to digest the food and pass the nutrients to the bloodstream. Each has limitations and dangers, but both have shown great promise in helping severely obese people lose weight rapidly and keep it off.

The most popular weight-loss surgery is Roux-en-Y gastric bypass surgery (GBS). GBS results in rapid and long-term weight loss with a minimal risk of dangerous side effects. Several celebrities, from Al Roker (*Today Show*) to Randy Jackson (*American Idol*), have turned to GBS to help them successfully reverse their weight problems. Many people feel uncomfortable seeking professional medical attention for obesity because they fear they will be treated as weak-willed and self-destructive. The success of GBS in celebrities has done much to help ease those fears. Public awareness has driven up the demand for the treatment, as people seeking a solution to obesity reach out for help.

Candidates for the surgery are carefully screened and must be at least a hundred pounds overweight in most cases. The procedure involves shrinking the size of the stomach by folding and stapling the stomach, leaving a greatly

Medicine has advanced to the point that many surgeries never thought possible are now becoming routine. Advances in surgery now allow doctors to perform procedures using extremely small and precise instruments. Some surgeries are performed almost entirely using a small video-scope called a laparoscope. A few very small incisions are all that are required to perform many surgeries with the use of the laparoscope. For most surgeries using this technology, recovery times, infection rates, and incidences of complications are all lower than when using traditional surgical methods.

reduced area for food. The surgeon shortens the upper section of the small intestine and attaches it to the pouch formed by the stapling of the stomach.

What results from the stapling and shortening process is that a much lower percentage of the food a person eats gets digested—and the individual's appetite is reduced because of the decreased amount of space for food. Normal, unmodified stomach volume can vary between fifty to sixty ounces, but a typical GBS patient will only be able to eat a few ounces of food at a time because the space simply does not exist for more. The significant reduction in stomach size means the patient will not be able to eat as much, and weight loss follows.

GBS patients must be careful because the surgery reduces the amount of all nutrients that get absorbed into the blood. A healthy diet can provide the vitamins and minerals vital to well-being, but this is not the case for those who have had GBS performed. A carefully balanced diet and daily nutritional supplements can alleviate the problem. Patients are advised to limit their intake of fatty or sweet foods after having the surgery.

Many patients who have GBS are very successful in their weight-loss effort. Most lose more than 50 percent of their excess weight and are able to keep it off for more than five years. Doctors estimate that an individual will lose as much as two-thirds of their excess weight within two years, and will keep the weight off for life.

Another option that requires a surgeon to reroute the digestive system is called biliopancreatic diversion (BPD). A more complicated procedure, BPD requires that the surgeon actually remove pieces of the stomach and stitch what remains together to form a smaller pouch, then attach it to the lower section of the small intestine. Nearly three-fourths of the small intestine is bypassed by the new routing. The main differences between BPD and GBS are the way the stomach is reduced and the amount of the small intestine

bypassed. BPD bypasses far more, further decreasing the uptake of fats by the body.

BPD is less common than GPS because of the invasive nature of the surgery and the increased incidence of side effects, such as severe vitamin deficiency. The removal of the majority of the small intestine from the digestive path prevents the body from absorbing many vitamins that are only found in fats. Multivitamin treatments do not always work, because there simply is not enough time for them to be absorbed into the bloodstream before the body expels them as waste.

Risks and Side Effects

Surgery is always risky, no matter what the procedure. Patients who do not qualify for *laparoscopic* techniques are at greater risk because the procedure requires opening the abdomen and exposing the internal organs. Scarring, hernias, and infection are among the more common risks of invasive surgery. Patients are warned to watch for signs of *bowel obstruction*, another possible consequence of the surgery. Neither malabsorptive surgery is reversible. What's done is done.

In addition to the medical complications arising from these surgeries, there is a risk the patient will suffer from long-term vitamin deficiency due to the reduced ability to absorb nutrients. Vitamin B-12, folate, and iron are commonly lost because they are taken up in the stomach and small intestine, which have been shortened by the surgery.

Many patients suffer from a postsurgery condition called dumping syndrome. A patient who eats excessively sugary food may experience severe abdominal cramping. Fatty foods cause instances of dumping because the upper part of the small intestine is very important in the normal digestive path for fats. The result is that they are not digested fully, and they are excreted undigested from the body.

When Malabsorptive Surgeries Don't Work

GBS is not foolproof by any means. Patients who refuse to change their diets often find they do not maintain the initial weight loss. Some people have adapted to the small stomach size by changing their eating habits, eating many small meals throughout the day, effectively taking in the same number of calories as they did before surgery—in spite of the reduced stomach size. Discipline is required for the treatment to work long term, and the burden is on the patient to maintain the weight loss.

Little can be done for a person who does not lose weight after such a procedure. Drug treatments will not be prescribed because of the fear of severe vitamin and mineral deficiencies. The only option that will likely remain is dieting, which may have failed the individual at least once in the past before she made the decision to undergo surgery.

Surgery may seem like a scary option—but your odds of dying from a weight-loss surgery are between one-tenth and three-tenths of one percent. That's about equal to your chances of being run over by an eighteen-wheel truck while walking along the side of a road. Most of us find those acceptable risks! And for most people, the benefits of weight-loss surgery more than outweigh the small risks. A study done in 2000 of five hundred patients showed that 96 percent of certain associated health conditions—such as back pain, sleep apnea, high blood pressure, diabetes, and depression—improved or disappeared after having weight-loss surgery.

A Surgical Patient

Scott lay on the gurney in his hospital gown, thinking about what brought him to this point. He had always thought he would be able to lose the extra weight easily enough; all he had to do was get to the gym and start eating a little less. He had made a New Year's resolution to change and had been slowly changing his diet.

No more chicken wings or pizza. Those were no-no's. Stop eating a whole bag of potato chips while watching television at night. Get up and take a walk. All these were things he had been planning on doing, sooner or later.

Chest pain made him change his plans. After a quick trip to the emergency room and treatment for angina, Scott was scared. He thought he was dying for sure. He made an appointment to see his family doctor.

The doctor found he had extremely high blood pressure and was at serious risk of heart problems. "Well, Scott," the doctor said, "looks like we dodged a bullet—but we might not be so lucky next time. I think it is time we had a talk about your weight."

The doctor had gone over several of the options with him, and they discussed the benefits and disadvantages of each. After much discussion, they concluded Scott needed to make a drastic change. He was not disciplined enough to lose weight and keep it off—and he was in desperate need of immediate weight loss. It was only a matter of time before he suffered a heart attack.

Scott and his doctor decided to go with gastric bypass surgery. *If it worked for Randy Jackson, it will work for me*, he thought as he lay on the gurney, hoping for a better life.

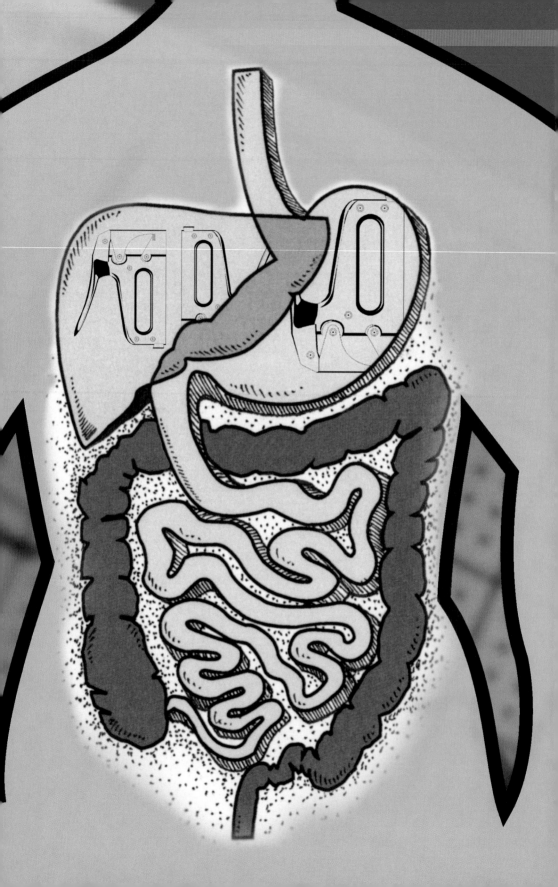

Chapter 7

Don't I Have Other Choices? I Like My Small Intestine!

- Restrictive Surgeries

- Success Rates

- Side Effects

No single treatment will work for every patient, so having options is critical to success. Some patients have preexisting conditions that will not allow doctors to use malabsorptive surgeries or drug therapies. For example, a patient with vitamin deficiency is not a good candidate for surgeries that change the way nutrients are absorbed. Doctors have to consider the health of the patient and use a treatment that will improve it.

Doctors have two surgical options for treating obesity that do not require significant cutting of the internal organs. While not as effective as the malabsorptive surgeries, they remain a valid option for people needing to control their weight.

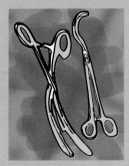

Restrictive Surgeries

Restrictive surgeries are exactly what they sound like. The goal of a restrictive surgery is to reduce—or restrict—the size of the stomach. Unlike malabsorptive surgeries, there is no rerouting of internal organs. Both methods of restrictive surgery create a much smaller stomach pouch, but do so without cutting into the organs.

The clear benefit of restrictive as opposed to malabsorptive surgeries is that they do not interfere with digestion in any way. The patient does not need to worry as much about vitamin deficiency because the section of the small intestine that is most important in absorbing vitamins remains intact and functional. Each piece of food a person eats is digested to the fullest extent, and as much nutrient as possible is absorbed.

Both of the restrictive surgeries reduce the stomach near the top, just below where the esophagus connects to it. Usually, the pouch created holds only a few ounces of food at one time, though it may stretch over time and hold slightly more. Typically, the pouch has a very small lower outlet that feeds the food into the rest of the stomach where digestion starts on protein and fats. The small outlet has the effect of causing the person to feel full and

remain that way for a while after eating. Food moves more slowly out of the pouch, and the cells of the stomach respond as though it were full, sending hormone messengers to the brain to make the person feel satisfied.

Adjustable gastric banding (AGB) is a procedure that restricts the size of the upper section of the stomach by wrapping a hollow band of special material around it. The band is filled with a salt solution to tighten it. Imagine holding a balloon and wrapping a rubber band around one end to create a smaller bubble. The effect of AGB is similar. The band can be adjusted, hence the name adjustable gastric banding. Over time, the bands may loosen or slip, and a simple incision allows the doctor to access the end of the tube to add fluid to the band, tightening it back up. The benefit of this type of surgery over others is that it can be fine-tuned after time has passed. It is not quite as final as the other types of weight-reduction surgery.

The other type of restrictive surgery is vertical gastric banding (VGB). A combination of staples and one band reduces the stomach size in this procedure. It is a more permanent change than the AGB, but it is free of the slippage that can affect the bands in the stomachs of AGB patients. VGB is more common than AGB because it is more reliable, but there are few true differences in effectiveness.

Success Rates

Patients having restrictive surgeries almost always lose significant weight soon after surgery. Nearly 30 percent of individuals who have restrictive surgery, either AGB or VGB, reach a healthy weight within two years and maintain the weight loss for long periods of time. Eighty percent of patients report at least some weight loss after surgery. Some patients have regained lost weight, mostly because they were unable to change their eating habits and caused stretching in the newly created stomach pouch. The success of restrictive surgeries depends on the patient maintaining a healthy lifestyle. Eating right and exer-

Between 1998 and 2001, less than one percent of all patients receiving a restrictive surgery were forced to return to the hospital to have a surgery to fix a slipped or leaking band.

cising regularly is the best way to make sure that the gains made as a result of this surgery last for life.

Side Effects

As is the case with many medical procedures, restrictive surgeries have several side effects. Some patients suffer from vomiting immediately after eating because they have eaten too much and their stomachs cannot stretch to accommodate the food. Large food particles caused by poorly chewed food can also cause vomiting. In addition, a person who consistently tries to eat more food than will fit in the pouch may suffer a condition called reflux, which causes feelings of nausea as the food backs up in the esophagus. The acid from the stomach can move up the esophagus and cause tiny ulcers to form in the esophagus; if the condition gets bad enough, the acid can enter the lungs and cause severe shortness of breath. Food that is not well chewed can have a similar effect, because it can block the narrow passage between the pouch and the rest of the stomach.

Some VGB patients have had to return to the hospital after reporting a burning sensation in their gut. On inspection, doctors found that the stapled areas of the stomach were leaking acid into the abdominal cavity, causing tissue damage. Emergency operations are required to plug the leaking area. Patients have also had to have the bands replaced because they have worn through from the vigorous motion of the stomach. Leaking bands are less of a concern because the salt solution pumped into them is not dangerous to the body in any way.

More serious complications have included abdominal infections requiring hospital stays and antibiotics, and the splitting of the stapled area of the stomach, which can cause the release of digestive enzymes and acid into the unprotected abdomen. A few deaths have occurred as a result of these more serious complications of the surgeries, but on the whole, these surgeries are very safe.

The success rate of restrictive surgery is lower than malabsorptive surgery, but the benefits are undeniable. For people who have other health conditions that make it very important for them to get all of the vitamins they can from their food, restrictive surgeries can be the next-best option. Many people have had great success with these surgical treatments, and the benefits to their health are likely to last them a lifetime.

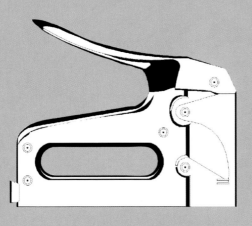

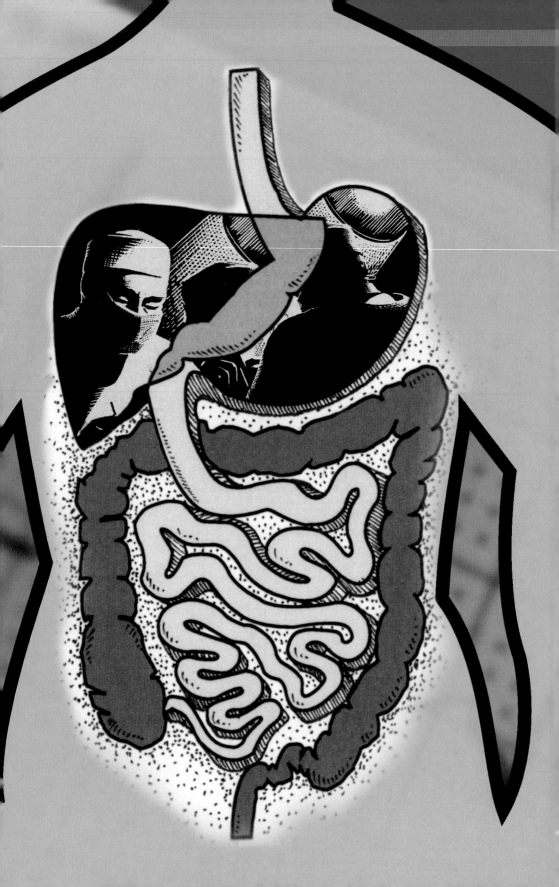

Chapter 8

What Else Is Left?

- Liposuction
- Tummy Tucks
- No Final Answers

Obesity is a health condition, not a cosmetic problem. However, our society places so much value on physical appearance that sometimes people worry more about how they look than about being healthy. As a result, several treatments exist that are solely cosmetic. A great deal of money is spent each year on surgeries intended to improve physical appearance.

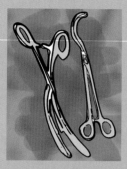

Liposuction

Liposuction may be the single most performed surgery that deals with fat. The name itself is a definition of what happens during the surgery. A doctor inserts a small tube through a tiny incision and sucks out the fat (lipids). The patient is usually given a strong anesthetic because the treatment can be very painful, since the majority of our nerve endings lie just under the skin, in the area where the tube is inserted. Sometimes a patient will receive a general anesthetic that knocks him out, especially if more than one area is to be treated. Most often the patient will receive an epidural, a strong anesthetic that blocks all feeling in the target area. The surgery is done in small outpatient clinics and can be performed very quickly. Most patients are in and out in a few hours.

The treatment is only temporary and is most often only intended as a quick-fix for problem areas where people have trouble losing fat. In areas that were stretched because of large amounts

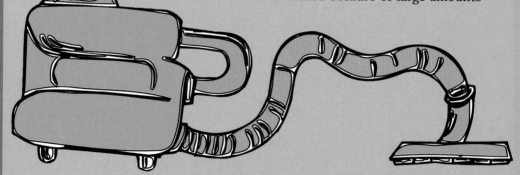

of fat, the skin sometimes hangs loosely, requiring more surgery to fix. A second procedure cuts the excess skin away. Cosmetic surgeries usually follow to reduce scarring in the treated areas. Liposuction patients are sometimes required to wear snug-fitting compression clothing to reduce swelling that occurs immediately after the surgery. Removing large amounts of fat can be

In 2003, there were 323,000 liposuctions performed. Of those, 80 percent were performed on women.

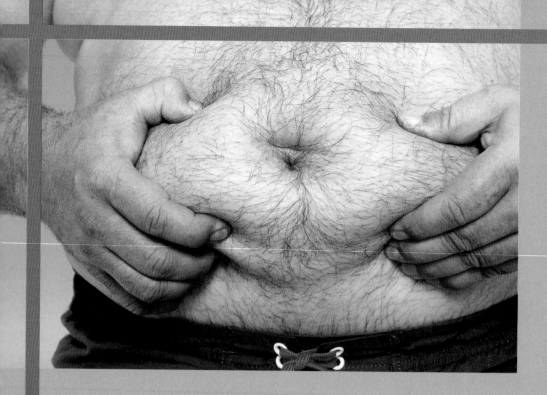

quite traumatic for the body, and the normal response includes swelling in the affected area. Swelling can lead to severe scarring, so doctors take steps to reduce or prevent it. Not all attempts are successful, and permanent scarring can occur.

Some patients experience a burning sensation under their skin in the treated area. In addition, there may be leakage of fluids in the areas that have had fat removed, including bleeding or oozing pus. Severe pain and soreness are common following the surgery, though a prescription for pain medication can help alleviate the problem.

As with all surgical procedures, patients should take their time and do their research in order to find a well-qualified doctor. With the increase in liposuction's popularity has come the increase in less than qualified people performing the procedure. Take the extra time to find the doctor who has a lot of experience with this type of procedure. Surgery is not a time when you want to be first in line.

Liposuction is not a true treatment for obesity. No long-term benefits to health have been documented, and repeat visits to the clinic are usually required over time. Many people turn to liposuction when they are desperate for a better look and are not willing to change their habits or seek true weight control. The gains are almost immediate and take little effort on the part of the individual.

Liposuction is not all bad though. Patients usually experience increases in self-confidence and can be inspired to change their lifestyle. Many patients begin to change their eating habits and take up some form of exercise in an effort to maintain their new look. Long-term health gains can follow as a result of the change.

Tummy Tucks

Abdominoplasty, or tummy tuck, is another cosmetic procedure used to remove excess fat from problem areas in people who are unable to lose it through more conventional means. A surgeon is required for this procedure, making it a major medical treatment. Most people wanting abdominoplasty have fat in common problem areas, such as the lower stomach and sides. The procedure removes excess skin and fat and can tighten abdominal muscles that have weakened over the years as a result of childbirth or lack of exercise.

A surgeon performing abdominoplasty makes a long incision into the

The number of tummy tucks increased by over 22 percent from 2002 to 2003.

abdominal wall and then pulls the skin tight, overlapping the sections and stitching the skin together to tighten and flatten the area. Often, the procedure leaves large scars. Some patients have scars that stretch from one hip to the other, but this depends on the amount of skin removed.

Like liposuction, the treatment is a temporary fix. Patients must change the way they eat and exercise in order for the treatment to last. Abdominoplasty can change a person's appearance immediately, but it is not likely to help long term for the same reasons as liposuction. The burden is on the patient to change his behavior, which can be very difficult.

Women who have given birth are the main candidates for abdominoplasty because the act of childbirth can stretch the abdominal muscles beyond their ability to recover. A woman needs to finish having her children before having the surgery, because additional childbirth can cause severe stretching, possibly even tearing of the abdominal wall.

Abdominoplasty is a true surgery and has many very real risks associated with it. Any time a scalpel is used, the risk of life-threatening infection and other complications increases. Patients have reported instances of slow healing, oozing scars, and severe pain. Most of the complications are not life threatening, but the possibility exists, so the patient must be aware.

No Final Answers

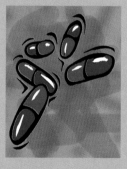

The changes that come with liposuction and abdominoplasty can be maintained for life if the patient is disciplined and can change her eating and exercise habits. These options, however, are never valid ways to manage weight. All other avenues for weight control should be tried before resorting to surgical treatment and the risks that come with it.

Obesity is a serious health condition that sometimes requires interventions such as medication or surgery. Usually, however, the best solution is to sim-

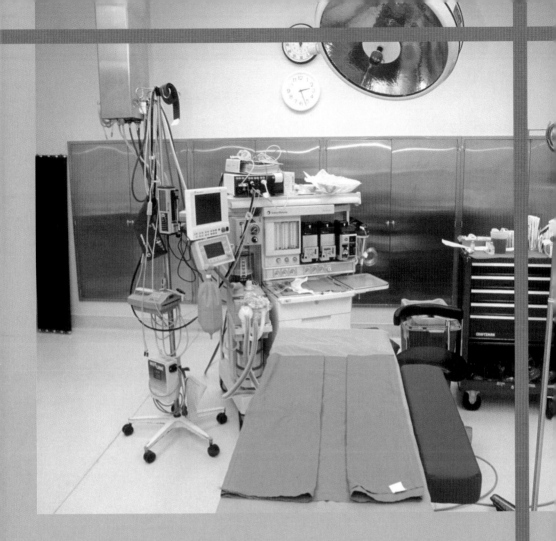

ply consume fewer calories while burning more. It does not take much to lose ten pounds each year. One less glass of soda a day can mean one hundred fewer calories taken in, which equals a loss of approximately ten pounds each year. Taking the stairs instead of the elevator is only one easy way to add more exercise to your life. With discipline and determination, we can all find ways to live a healthier lifestyle.

But whether diet and exercise is all it takes—or medication and surgery—good health should always be a person's ultimate goal. In the long run, appearances don't count for very much. Being healthy does.

A Disappointing Surprise

Keisha's father was a doctor, and her mother was an attorney. They never worried too much about money, and Keisha's parents usually gave her anything she requested. She wasn't spoiled rotten, because she wasn't rotten, but she probably was a little bit spoiled.

Keisha knew what she wanted for her eighteenth birthday. She had been thinking about it for months, or maybe even years. She'd spent her whole life feeling like she was fat and unappealing, and she intended to do something about it. She'd watched those plastic surgery shows where women got all the fat sucked out of their bellies. Liposuction! That would be the answer to all her problems.

Her parents weren't thrilled with the idea, but they eventually agreed. Keisha couldn't wait. She knew it wouldn't be very much fun, but she was certain it would be worth it. The doctor talked to her about all the risks, but she was too excited to listen.

The day dawned, misty and damp, but the rain didn't dampen Keisha's spirit. Today was the day she was going to be thin!

Keisha woke up after the surgery, feeling groggy, disconnected, and a bit like she had been in a car wreck.

She hurt pretty much everywhere, even places she knew they hadn't touched.

Several days later, Keisha was still recuperating at home, taking it pretty easy and spending most of the time in bed with a book or watching TV. She was swollen, and she was surprised at how lumpy and odd her stomach looked.

After a couple weeks, the swelling had gone down, but Keisha's body still looked weird. She went back to the doctor for a check-up, and he told her that there had been a problem with the procedure. Her skin probably wasn't going to go back to normal, and she might be lumpy for the rest of her life.

She couldn't believe it. She thought liposuction would make her skinny and beautiful. Instead it left her worse off than she started!

Glossary

anorexia nervosa: An eating disorder characterized by a distorted body image and an inability to maintain a healthy body weight because of failure to eat.

bile: A digestive fluid produced in the liver and stored in the gallbladder.

binge eat: To eat a large amount of food at one time, often followed by purging.

bowel obstruction: A blockage in a section of the intestine that hinders elimination.

bulimia: An eating disorder in which periods of overeating are followed by periods of undereating or self-induced vomiting or use of laxatives.

clinical studies: A series of scientific research studies conducted to see if a drug works and what possible side effects there might be.

convulsions: Episodes of violent shaking of the body or limbs caused by uncontrollable muscle contractions.

dehydration: A loss of body fluids.

diabetics: People who have diabetes, a disease caused by an inefficient use or production of insulin.

diuretics: Drugs that cause an increased output of urine.

dopamine: A chemical found in the brain that transmits nerve impulses.

enzyme: A protein produced by living cells that promotes a specific biochemical reaction.

epidemic: An outbreak of a disease or medical condition that spreads more quickly and more extensively than would be expected.

extract: Something that is removed from something else.

gallbladder: A small sac on the underside of the liver where bile is stored until it is needed in the digestive process.

hernias: Conditions in which part of an internal organ projects abnormally though the wall of the cavity in which it is contained.

hormones: Chemicals produced in the endocrine glands or certain other glands that have a regulatory or stimulatory effect.

laparoscopic: Involving a laparoscope, a fiberoptic instrument inserted through the abdominal wall.

mass produce: To make something in large quantities and all the same.

menopause: The time in a woman's life during which she stops menstruating.

metabolism: Ongoing chemical interactions that provide the energy and nutrients necessary to sustain life.

morbidly: Having the characteristics of a disease.

prejudiced: To have opinions (usually bad ones) based on insufficient knowledge or inaccurate information, often based on racial, ethnic, or physical characteristics.

receptors: Things that receive the action of others.

saturated fat: Fat that comes from animal products.

stigma: The shame attached to something that is regarded socially unacceptable.

stimulant: A drug or other chemical that produces a temporary increase in the functioning of a body organ.

Further Reading

Brownell, Kelly D. and Katherine Battle Horgen. *Food Fight: The Inside Story of the Food Industry, America's Obesity Crisis, and What We Can Do About It.* Chicago: McGraw-Hill, 2003.

Fumento, Michael. *The Fat of the Land: The Obesity Epidemic and How Overweight Americans Can Help Themselves.* New York: Viking Books, 1997.

Hochstrasser, April and S. Ross Fox. *The Patient's Guide to Weight Loss Surgery: Everything You Need to Know About Gastric Bypass and Bariatric Surgery.* Long Island City, N.Y.: Hatherleigh Press, 2004.

Martin, Louis F. *Obesity Surgery.* New York: McGraw-Hill, 2003.

Mitchell, Deborah R. *The Diet Pill Book: A Consumer's Guide to Prescription and Over-the-Counter Weight Loss Pills and Supplements.* New York: St. Martin's Press, 2002.

Peck, Paula F. *Exodus from Obesity: The Guide to Long-Term Success After Weight Loss Surgery.* New York: BP Publishing Inc., 2003.

Pool, Robert. *Fighting the Obesity Epidemic.* New York: Oxford University Press, 2001.

Richards, Byron J. *Mastering Leptin.* Minneapolis, Minn.: Wellness Resources Books, 2003.

Rinzler, Carol Anne. *Weight Loss Kit for Dummies.* New York: Hungry Minds Inc., 2001.

Shelton, Ron M. and Terry Malloy. *Liposuction: A Question-and-Answer Guide to Today's Most Popular Cosmetic Procedure.* New York: Berkley Publishing Group, 2004.

For More Information

Aim for a Healthy Weight
www.nhlbi.nih.gov/health/public/heart/obesity/lose_wt/index.htm

American Obesity Association
www.obesity.org/

Appetite-Wikipedia
en.wikipedia.org/wiki/Appetite

FDA—What Is Liposuction
www.fda.gov/cdrh/liposuction/what.html

From the Cleveland Clinic: Is Weight Loss Surgery For You?
my.webmd.com/content/article/46/2731_1656

From the Cleveland Clinic: Prescription Weight Loss Medicine
my.webmd.com/content/article/46/2731_1668

Gastric Surgery for Severe Obesity
www.niddk.nih.gov/health/nutrit/pubs/gastric/gastricsurgery.htm

Guide to Prescription Weight Loss Drugs
www.healthyweightforum.org/eng/weight_loss_medication/

KidsHealth—Weight-Loss Surgery and Teens
kidshealth.org/research/weight_loss_surgery.html

Obesity Drug Leptin Shows Promise
www.applesforhealth.com/leptindrug1.html

Obesity Drug Treatment: Weight Loss
www.weight-loss-i.com/obesity-drug-treatment-weight-loss.htm

Obesity Treatment Options: Gastric Bypass and Weight Loss Surgery
www.weightlosssurgeryinfo.com/pages/treatments/index.jsp

OMNI—Obesity
omni.ac.uk/browse/mesh/C0028754L0028754.html

Prescription Medications for the Treatment of Obesity
www.niddk.nih.gov/health/nutrit/pubs/presmeds.htm

Weight Loss for Life
www.niddk.nih.gov/health/nutrit/pubs/wtloss/wtloss.htm

Weight Loss Programs, Diet Pill, Surgery, and Weight Loss Diets
www.weight-loss-i.com/

Publisher's note:
The Web sites listed on these pages were active at the time of publication. The publisher is not responsible for Web sites that have changed their addresses or discontinued operation since the date of publication. The publisher will review the Web sites and update the list upon each reprint.

Index

Biographies

William Hunter lives in western New York with his wife, Miranda. Bill graduated from Fredonia University with a B.S. in biology and the University at Buffalo with an M.A. in biology. Bill and his wife have written several other nonfiction books for young adults, including *Staying Safe: A Teen's Guide to Sexually Transmitted Diseases*.

Dr. Victor F. Garcia is the co-director of the Comprehensive Weight Management Center at Cincinnati Children's Hospital Medical Center. He is a board member of Discover Health of Greater Cincinnati, a fellow of the American College of Surgeons, and a two-time winner of the Martin Luther King Humanitarian Award.

Picture Credits

Banana Stock: pp. 33, 37, 66
Comstock: p. 20
Corbis: pp. cover (lower right), 52, 53
Corel: p. 12
Clipart.com: pp. 14, 61, 64, 75, 87, 97
Imagesource: p. 26
Photo Disc: pp. cover (upper left), cover (upper right), 17, 19 24
Photos.com: pp. cover (lower left), 23, 67, 76, 77, 83, 85, 95
Stockbyte: p. 11